To Gigi, who always supported my love for poetry

Table of Contents

Section I — 7
If You Squint Your Eyes — 8
Look Up! — 9
An Inferno Storm — 10
A Dance of Chaos — 11
The Beautiful Sunset — 12
Paint The Sky — 13
Chaos — 14
A Split In The Road — 15-16
Tempest — 17
Nature Is Art — 18
Autumn's Harvest — 19
The Artist of Fall — 20
Fall's Reminder — 21
Spooky Season — 22
A Witches' Whisper — 23
Roses — 24
Sinister — 25
Nature's Icy Warning — 26
Gracefully — 27
A Woven Story — 28
Winter <3 — 29
A Wintry Reflection — 30
The Season of Ice — 31
An Illusion — 32
Forever Winter — 33
Nature's Tango — 34
Her Long Reign — 35
Melting — 36
The Time Between — 37
Sisters of the Land — 38-39
Without — 40
The Goddess of the Hunt — 41

Hekate	*42*
Selene	*43*
The Wood Nymphs	*44*
The Naiad's Song	*45*
The Willows	*46*
Cross Roads	*47*
Love	*48*
A Sea of Green	*49*
Intertwined	*50*
Tides	*51*
Not A Fool	*52*
Incandescent	*53*
Silence	*54*
Will It?	*55*
Time Slips Away	*56*
Hourglass	*57-58*
Golden Illusion	*59*
Change	*60*
????	*61*
I Miss You	*62*
Away	*63*
Section II	**64**
Eerie Silence of Night	*65*
The Things I Love	*66*
Daughter of The Moon	*67*
Enchanted	*68*
The Moon's Love	*69*
The Sun's Love	*70*
A Love They'll Never Have	*71*
Eclipse	*72*
Cycle of Endings	*73*
Always and Forever	*74*
Stars Above & Love	*75*
I'd Give You The Moon	*76*
Enervated	*77*

Watching the Sun Dance with the Moon	78
Ignorance Isn't Bliss	79
If I Wanted The Moon	80
The Midnight Sky	81
Constellations?	82
Starry Eyed	83
A Sea of Mysteries	84
Stars	85
The Gentle Stars	86
Losing Someone	87
Shooting Stars	88
Wishes For the Future	89
Silly Wishes	90
Wish	91
Longing	92
Meant To Be	93
Turning Nothing Into Something	94
Nonsense?	95
Day Falls to Night	96
Yule	97
Section III	**98**
Fate	99
The Small Things	100
A Little Less Wiser	101
Inevitable Change	102
Memories Veiled in Ivory	103
What Once Was	104
A Release of Time	105
Promises of Time	106
Waiting For Time	107
A Cursed Truth	108-109
Unwise	120
What's The Point?	111
The Stories in Lines	112
Unimaginative	113

Time	*114*
Like Snow	*115*
Past, Present, and Future	*116*
Section IV	**117**
The Little Things I Favor	*118*
An Answer of Why	*119*
Home	*120*
Unspoken Words	*121*
I Love You	*122*
I'll Cherish Your Love	*123*
To Be Loved	*124*
A Love That'll Last	*125*
Those I Love	*126*
Photography	*127*
Ominous	*128*
A Star's Disappearance	*129*
The Veil Between	*130*
You're Not The Sun	*131*
An Ocean of Emotion	*132*
Failing To See	*133*
Opposition	*134*
What More?	*135*
What You Couldn't Say	*136*
Eyes	*137*
A Hazy Heart	*138*
Why?	*139*
You	*140*
A Final Goodbye	*141*
Once Had	*142*
Too Much	*143*
Never A Mistake	*144*
Forgiveness	*145*
Haunted	*146*
If Only You'd Listen	*147*
Depths of Your Mind	*148*

Death	*149*
The Silence of Death	*150*
A Midnight Stroll	*151*
A Kingdom of Darkness	*152*
Castle of Midnight	*153-154*
The Sea, The Monster & The Night	*155*
The Valkyrie's Armor of Light	*156*
What's Above	*157*
This Sea of Voices	*158*

Section I

Nature

If You Squint Your Eyes...

If you squint your eyes just enough, you should be able to see through the cloudy haze that blocks your vision.

If you squint your eyes just enough you'll see things anew.

If you squint your eyes just enough you'll begin to see the world you cannot, when your eyes are fully open.

If you squint your eyes just enough you will see that the sky is a deep violet. Not blue.

If you squint your eyes just enough the ocean isn't blue, it's a dark teal, the shade of the night's sky.

If you squint your eyes just enough the trees don't stay still, they sway, and morph into things you've never seen.

If you squint your eyes just enough, you should be able to see through the cloudy haze that blocks your vision.

Look Up!

If you look up, look at the sky.
The clouds scatter the sky.
Like a shield from the sun.
The hue of the sky,
So beautiful
So vibrant.
So,
If you look up, look at the sky.

An Inferno Storm

Looking up at the sky,
I think of how blue,
It looks to me.
Clouds begin to roll in,
As I let out a sigh,
From where I stand, it's true-
The sky is blue, but far from the sea-
The sky looks yellow; a storm taking form.
Fires from the north bring in smoke,
Covering the land in a foggy cloak.

A Dance of Chaos

A storm is brewing in the dark sky.
Dancing with the trees, the wind sighs,
Always stuck in an elaborate dance,
as beautifully intricate as a royal scheme.

Painting the scene in a white light,
the divine lighting takes a stance,
as rain pelts violent, raging streams.

Clouds block the sun, creating a false night.
This story is one full of chaos,
though, from afar it is quite serene.

The Beautiful Sunset

The sun will set with grace.
It will paint the sky, all vibrant colors.
Every color blending into the next
Creating a haunting painting.

The stars will slowly appear,
Shining bright like fairy lights, you'd hang on your wall.

The breeze gently pushes through the trees.
It breaks the peaceful silence.
Creating a soft melody.

The water's current gently crashes into the rocks.
The sound adds onto the wind's melody.
Creating a beautiful song, to go along with the beautiful scenery.

Paint The Sky

Sometimes, I'd like to paint the sky,
put it down on a canvas,
and try to make something as simple-
as the setting sun, more beautiful-
than poetic words can describe.
Though, I'll never get around-
to painting the evening sky,
I'll always watch out for the sunset.
Watch as it creates a story,
one I will never know.

Chaos

The calm before the storm,
presents the huge swarm,
of clouds that cover the river.

Warning those on the land-
of the storm that's brewing.
The frozen, undisturbed sand-
looks as if it was spun from sugar.

The storm refuses to falter,
as it rains down on the beautiful flowers,
The wind's full of laughter, as it showers-
the land with light rain as the trees sway.

Curious nymphs watch the storm,
their attention never straying-
from the roar of thunder, as lighting forms.

A Split In the Road

A crack in the road,
A scratch in the glass,
Isn't the end of the world.
For every "imperfection,"
Beauty is made.

In that crack in the road-
Flowers and trees can grow.
In that scratch in the glass,
There is a ray of light, that slowly will pass,
As the sun begins to set.
When two new roads have met,
You can decide which one to take.
There's nothing beauty cannot make.

Deep into the heart of winter,
When everything appears dead,
The icicles hanging from the trees-
Gleam in the evening sunlight.
The snow trickles down from the sky,
As the wind exhales, almost a sigh.

Late into the hot summer nights,
The moon shines so bright,
Casting its gentle glow onto the land.
Meanwhile, in the winter,
It reflects off of the false sand.

When the land begins to dance with icy winds,
Fall paints the landscape in reds and oranges, like a fire.
The complete opposite of spring,
Whose green thumb grows flowers of many colors.

Tempest

Listening to the wind sing,
I watch clouds form a ring,
A storm begins to brew,
as the sky becomes anew.
Thunder rolls in,
demanding to be heard,
the storm starts to begin.
Everything becomes unfettered.
The world spins into turmoil,
as rain starts to pelt the soil.

Nature Is Art

Little green, red, and orange trees paint the bottom of the canvas.
Mountains and hillsides too, paint the bottom of the canvas.
Rivers, ponds, and lakes scatter across the Earth like cracks in a sculpture.
The ocean waves crash against the shore, like music played in a band.
Clouds are clay, they shift and mold into shapes.
The seasons paint different scenes of a story.
The sunset colors the sky with purples, pinks, oranges, and blues.
 Nature is art.

Autumn's Harvest

As the years go by,
the seasons may become a blur,
but late in the evenings of autumn,
you'll hear the wind start to sigh.
Time feels as if it began to stir
as the harvest moon shines high in the sky.
The cold seeps into the ground
as word begins to go around
that winter is on its way.
The animals know it too,
as they huddle together, snug like a bug.
Burrowed deep into the ground like a potato,
rabbits hide from the warnings of winter.

The Artist of Fall

When night awakes sooner,
and the stars become brighter,
Fall descends onto the land.
Soon enough, winter will bring its false sand,
until then, the leaves paint the sky-
as the trees and wind begin to sigh.
There's a slight chill to the air,
as clouds peer down at the land without a care.
Fall dances with life and death,
as it slowly kills the once green leaves.
With this new death, it'll bring new life.
Fall gently whisks away the last of Summer's-
gentle warmth from the land, preparing-
the animals for the winter that's raging-
on the horizon, bringing its cold.
Fall paints the landscape beautifully,
throwing yellows, oranges, and reds onto-
the portrait it's trying to paint, bold-
blues and purples paint the horizon,
as the sun begins to quickly set,
showing the eager stars, as they glow.
Fall paints the chilly breeze in misty grays-
as it knows the morning fog will paint-
the land in a ghostly pale white curtain,
that'll haunt the mornings until Fall,
always the selective artist, is satisfied with its art.

Fall's Reminder

The stars begin to realign,
Opening new doors,
As summer starts to resign.
With whispers of love anew,
Fall changes what we once knew.
Bringing us a new gentleness.
One made out of love,
One that touches the ocean shores,
And stretches to the mountains.
Where leaves fall in heaps, like fountains.

Fall shows us the beauty in change,
Hoping we'll accept it rather than think it strange.
As a refreshing crisp settles into the air,
The sun sets without a care.
With night growing darker,
The fiery trees disappear into the shadows.
Clouds gather above like silky meadows.
Fall gives a soft reminder,
Hoping we'll open our minds –
To what's in front of us.

Spooky Season

When the air is crisp,
with a chilly breeze,
Fall puts a spell on me.

The leaves fall in a wisp,
as an artist weaves-
a portrait of the fiery sea.

Though, it's not February,
love seeps through the air.
For all things spooky, and scary,
as we celebrate autumn without a care.

Bats fly above ours heads, as night-
falls, casting the stars a glow.
They are the land's spooky light,
as we enjoy our time before the snow.

A Witches' Whisper

Whispers of the wind brush past me,
Kicking up the fiery leaves,
As the trees begin to make a sea-
of dead leaves, creating a painting that weaves-
Its own story as dark clouds begin to roll in.

There's a chill to the evening air,
as a holiday approaches, it spins-
the once peaceful breeze into a warning,
of things that should not exist.

As witches cast a spell on the land.
Their chant echoes through the forest,
a sound so enchanting-
the most steel-hearted person-
wouldn't resist their sweet melody.

Dancing with the gentle full moon,
their laughter fills the woods.
As warm as the sun, their fire-
glows bright, promising a winter full of warmth.

Roses

The world is a rose,
it is quite beautiful,
but its thorns hurt.
The wind sings songs of gold,
that never seem to mold,
but behind each pretty lyric,
is a warning you should listen to.
Except, it's not something you hold onto,
So you let it pass,
like the ticking time.
The sea is deadly,
but you only listen to its melody.
Thunder calls out warnings,
that you don't listen to until the mornings.

Sinister

A storm is brewing ahead,
as everything falls dead,
the leaves are no longer green,
and the sun cannot be seen.
Dark clouds cover the blue sky,
as the wind kisses the land like a sigh.
In the heart of the woods,
ice seeps into everything good.

The trees are now bare,
and time stills without a care.
The threat of winter is on the horizon,
it's similar to the way the sun-
sets for the dark, unforgiving night;
they will snuff out everything that may be light.

Nature's Icy Warning

Storms warn what's ahead,
Icy hugs from the wind above,
as winter rolls in.

Gracefully

Snow gracefully
falls down onto
the still land.

A strong wind
pushes the
frozen trees.

Howling wind,
fills the empty
silence of the land.

As the animals
slumber, a fire
cracks and sizzles.

The warmth of
the fire competes
with the frigid air.
Creating a serene,
feeling of love.

A Woven Story

With a story only the wind knows,
I watch in dead silence as the snow,
falls onto the land, engulfing it in a hug.
Each snowflake dances in the icy air,
as animals come closer; warm and snug.

Fall passed us without a single care,
leaving us with winter's pale eyes of blue.
The sun sets in hues of golden yellow,
On this mountain, the land below is a view-
unlike any other; everything seems mellow.

Calm and serene, almost as if time listens-
to winter, who's tears practically glisten,
in the gentle star light of the quiet night,
everything is still as if time is frozen.
Winter is a true masterpiece, woven-
to absolute perfection, without a flaw.

Winter <3

When the butterflies leave for the south,
the cold begins to seep through,
when the leaves fall,
The frost begins to cover everything in view.

As the snow covers the ground,
no animal makes a sound.
The chilly breeze,
brushes past the trees,
shaking off the light snow,
dusting the animals below.

When the sun sets,
the stars begin to shine,
and the animals below.
sleep with no frets.

When the sun rises,
it reflects off of the snow,
glistening like glitter.
The sun comprises,
a gentle warmth.

A Wintry Reflection

When the wind is an icy hug,
and the snow is a blanket, holding the ground snug,
when the trees no longer sway, rocking back and forth,
and a fire is ablaze next to a comforting hearth,
it feels as if everything stops.

Time itself is now frozen, stuck in winter's trance.
Winter, a time of reflection, though at first glance-
It seems as if it's nothing but a dreadful season.

When the snow falls, that's when the fun begins,
as sheets of ice become a natural mirror, with a reason-
that must be found in the heart of the cold, as the world spins.
Although the land is wrapped in a bitter hug,
the mortals who roam, live happily and snug.

The Season of Ice

As a child, I would watch the snow melt-
and no matter how I felt-
I knew all good things must come to an end.

Winter was my favorite season,
snow gently falling onto my face,
like cold, tiny kisses from the sky.
And, I would always wonder why-
no one else favored winter too.
I never cared for the cold,
but when the sun set-
it wrapped around me in a tight hold.

As a teenager, I would watch the snow melt-
and no matter how I felt-
I knew all good things must come to an end.

Winter is my favorite season.
I love the slowly falling snow.
Winter has never felt like my foe-
so I always wonder why-
as I look up at the cloudy sky-
Why does no one else favor winter, too?
I will never care for the cold,
as it freezes my fingers-
together in a tight hold,
but I will always love the icy season,
and for so many reasons.

An Illusion

I love winter,
enjoying every single part.
Though, its icy embrace is like a splinter.
One I cannot seem to get out,
As it sinks deep within my heart,
seeping through my body.

I begin to wonder if its beauty is real.
I wonder if it's an illusion,
an elaborate one that's captured my eye.
And with each melodic sigh,
I breathe it in, not wanting to see through it.
Not wanting to see what may be true.

Forever Winter

When the sun looks down at the land,
The winter snow takes a stand.
Without a word, the world stills.
Refusing to melt into nothing,
The snow ignores the sun's far from loving-
brimmingly brutal, burning, stare.
This fight has gone on, for far too long,
The wind and the sea barely sing a song-
This long, but the snow continues to stand.
As the sun continues to glare.

Nature's Tango

Snow dances around the land,
as the wind tries to keep up
with its slow, deliberate tempo.

Trees sway back and forth,
joining the snow's dance.
Stars above twinkle,
casting their gentle glow
onto the white sand.

The snow begins to erupt,
into a breathtaking fiasco.
They continue to dance, as they move north.

The snow's movements advance,
As the tree branches begin to crinkle,
the wind falters, losing its flow.

Her Long Reign

When the Summer dies,
Fall begins to descend,
onto the beloved land.
With no words, and no ties-
Winter sinks its teeth into the sand.

Leaving nothing to mend.
Deep into the cruel season,
love leaves without reason.
Winter's heart of ghastly ice-
leaves us scrambling like mice.

Spring will not come for us soon,
it'll wait five, treacherous full moons,
before dancing with the winter wind.
Sweeping up the scintillating snow.

Then Spring will abruptly leave us,
we'll, once again, be left with Winter,
and her heart of ruthless ice.
Though, we'll no longer be scrambling mice.

Melting

There is no cloud in sight,
to block out the setting sun's light.
The sun's rays reflect off of the snow.
Lighting up the wintery sand.
Silence fills the air, but there's no doe-
in sight, on this sun kissed land.

The Time Between

In the dead of winter,
crows call out,
their song a splinter-
in the silence of doubt.
Spring is longed for.
Its warmth wanted more-
than ever before.

Though, in the time between,
beauty can be seen.
Winter's icy breath,
is as silent as death.
As time slowly stills,
waiting for spring's hills-
of flowers that draw in the rain.
As the chilly air is all that remains-
of winter's comforting embrace,
when there's only spring's grace.

Sisters of the Land

In most stories, there's only two sides.
Though, that is not the case here.
Four sisters rule the land side by side.
The eldest, Winter, rules with a heart of ice.
As her little sister, Spring creates a sea,
In hopes it'll look extravagantly nice-
to the humans Summer watches over.
As she impatiently waits for her turn-
to rule, as she keeps their fires ablaze.

Fall, the most quiet one of them all, paints the leaves,
as if she takes the beautiful colors and weaves-
them into the plants; like fire ready to burn.
Winter crafts intricate mazes-
ready to build the sisters a palace.
Summer, though, is full of malice.
As she and Spring will slowly melt the sculpture.

Unlike her sisters, Fall is like a vulture-
ready to find something new to have-
or somewhere new to simply be.
Spring quickly creates her own castle-
moving as far East as she can.
Summer follows suit, moving South in a hurry.
Fall, unwilling to stay in one spot leaves her sister to stand-

alone as she rules in a cloud of worry.

Though, Winter's heart is one of ice.
She knows how her sisters are like mice.
Winter knows, they'll eventually come back.
Until then, Winter rules the unforgiving North,
Spring rules the frigid, flowery East,
Summer rules the humid South,
and Fall rules the beautiful West.

Without

Without the warmth of Summer,
Winter would be loved.
Without the quiet breeze of Fall,
Spring's rainy days would be adored.
Without one, there wouldn't be the other.

The Goddess of The Hunt

She watches the land,
watching the animals,
as they scurry around.
She waits for her prey,
hunting is her speciality,
her arrows never miss,
each one striking its
target perfectly.
She has no fear,
of what's in the woods,
nymphs of all kinds,
accompany her.
She is a protector,
a force to be
reckoned with.
She is no fool.
She is as fierce as the
wolves that roam the
quiet woods.
She is;
The Goddess of The Hunt.

Hekate

At midnight,
when everything is vast asleep,
shadows and creatures lurk about,
hidden crossroads appear,
out of thin air.

Underneath the pale moonlight,
no human dares venture
into the shadow filled woods.
Where a goddess disguised
as a witch brews up a spell.

A small polecat brushes up against her leg,
not bothered by the sleeping beasts,
The goddess's hounds slumber,
snuggling close to the warm hearth.
Snakes coil themselves around her arms,
showing their affection to the goddess of witchcraft.

In the small little cottage,
the goddess resides in,
during her time in the upper world.
Many believe the goddess to be evil,
as revengeful as she can be,
She cares for those who are lost.

Selene

Late at night,
The owls sing.
With no light,
there's no king

to rule over
the sleeping land.
The moon goddess
watches the land.

High in the
sky, she watches.
Quiet as a
mouse, she is.

She gazes down,
looking on the
snow covered land,
the frozen town,
covered in sand.

The Wood Nymphs

When the sun sets,
And the moon is high in the sky,
The naiads swim to the surface-
of their watery home.

The moon's pale light reflects-
off of the sea of stone,
They look out past their home.
On the land, instead of sand, sits-
a forest full of slumbering trees.

Moss covers each and every tree
like a soft, green blanket.
They stare in awe at the dryads-
as they grow oak trees in seconds.

In the pale moonlight, the dryads'
moss green skin looked like sea glass.
As time quickly passed, the dryads disappeared-
into their homes, high in the oak trees.

The Naiad's Song

In the evening, on a rainy day,
The willow trees weep.
Underneath the willows, dryads stay.
They are peaceful as they sleep.

Wind pushes the willows as rain-
gently hits the ground, naiads sing.
Their voices; a peaceful sound.
The Dryad's hear their alluring melody.

The once slumbering, Dryads listen,
As the rain softens, the naiads hum.
The willows no longer weep, as the-
rain slowly disappears, and glistens-
off of the dim light, as the air numbs.

The Willows

I long for that warm feeling,
but not in the form I already know.
I am well versed in its song,
full of unspoken lyrics
I know by heart,
The words are engraved in my head.

I long for the song of the Willow Tree,
when the wind dances with its branches.
A song of mystery, it is.
I want to listen closely,
to hear its wisdom in song.

I wish for the song of the Willow
to be engraved in my head;
for it to be a song I know by heart.
I don't fear what lies beyond
The mystery of the Willow Tree song.

If I wish to hear the song of the Willows,
I must hear the entirety of its graceful song.
Until the Willows sing their song to me,
I am left longing for their angelic melody.

Cross Roads

Our roads cross,
fate set in the stars.
When will our roads split?
Love written in the sea,
wind dancing with the storm.
Clinging to hope like moss,
We didn't see what was ours.
There's no landslide to flee,
whispers begin to swarm.
Oh, when will worry let us be?
Bittersweet like the snow,
only the stars know.
What awaits us is a mystery,
one that'll be left behind in our history.

Love

Love can take many forms.
It appears in the way the moon,
is drawn to the sea, creating storms-
showing their love, that won't leave anytime soon.

It appears in the way the sun,
hugs the sky as it sets, silently making a promise,
as the sky begins to let the colors run,
allowing the land to see the sun's unbroken promise.

It appears in the way water engulfs fire-
creating a strong pull between the two,
as smoke begins to climb higher-
into the sky, as they always do.

Its hold over nature will forever last,
always creating a beautiful symphony.

A Sea of Green

When the moon shines the brightest,
the vines that wrap around-
the trees, move out of sight
Just when I think they might-
shrivel down to green moss,
they turn into green daisies,
surrounding me in a sea-
of a beautiful green.

Intertwined

When only the stars shine,
the winds' whispered rhyme-
echoes across the land.
As the sea longs for the moon.

The magnetic pull-
Weaves their fates together.
Intertwining them for eternity.

The moon chases the earth,
as the sea reaches up,
Forever trying to find each other.

Tides

Drawn like a magnet,
the moon and the sea.
Water reaching for light,
stars shining in the night,
watching as the moon-
pulls away,
steering the water astray.

Not A Fool

You always wait until the moon disappears,
before looking up at the stars,
now seeing them for how beautiful they are.
Without the moon, the sea knows how vain
you truly are, but you are merely a shadow forged
from light.
A light, that is 'too bright,' for the sea.
On cloudy days, when the sea's waves crash against
the shore
You can hear its despondent song, and its vexed
tone.
"Why must it rain-
for you to see *my* pain?
Dear, I shine *just* as bright,
as the moon's soft light.
Why must it pour-
for *you* to end this silent war?
Dear, I am as striking
as the gentle moon.
So I will ask again;
Why must it rain-
for you to see *my* pain?"
The sea is no fool, as you like to claim.
This is not a foolish game,
for you to win, leaving the sea in shame.

Incandescent

In the late evenings,
in a pool of fire-
There lies a liar.
Living on this land,
all they cared about-
was the pitiful sand.
They ignore the flames,
and point fingers-
to find who's to blame.

Silence

The rain washes away,
everything the sun touched,
ripping the warmth of the day,
from those who desperately clutched-
onto the golden rays of sweet summer.
Once the rain comes to a halting stop,
you'll hear the wind's deep slumber,
as its snores echo off the silent land.
Leaving you haunted by what once was.

Will It?

Will the rain wash away-
the ash of today?
Water reflects the land-
that's fragile like sand.

Do you really understand?
Will the promise of tomorrow,
keep the world from sorrow?
Or must we continue to borrow,
from what isn't ours?

All of the days short hours,
will be gone in the blink of an eye.
And soon the moon will be high in the sky.

Time Slips Away

The ancient moon
has many stories to tell,
though the sun takes the bell.
Years feel as if they slip by
like sand in an hourglass.

Day turns to night, grass
turns to leaves, as fall lies
on your doorstep, though,
in the south, winter rules, casting
the land in ice, as snow begins to grow.

As time goes by, the land is forever changing.
Fearing nothing, winter engulfs everything.
When fall leaves, and winter knocks on your door,
you'll feel as if summer leaves too soon.

Hourglass

At dusk,
the birds quiet,
and the trees
still, like statues,

stars appear through
the clouds like
little pieces of
silver confetti.

The moon rises,
casting its light
onto the
sleeping land.

Water ripples across
lakes of stone,
with the moon
reflecting off
the smooth surface.

The humans slumber
as the moon

flies across the
land of sand.

Time flies by
and slips through
many hands.

Golden Illusion

Fell in love with a golden illusion.
World veiled in a bronze light,
Everything felt right.

The warmth of sun kissing skin,
The reassurance of night,
The ease brought by a breeze.

This enchanting illusion soon shattered,
With the cold seeping into the night,
Changing as if nothing else mattered.

The land afire from afar,
With only the suns quick descent,
To bring along the calm.

Hiding this gentle reminder;
Nothing ever lasts forever.

Change

My life is changing
like the four seasons,
though without any reason —
I find myself scared of it.
Change, it's a horrifying but beautiful thing.
Like in the early mornings of spring,
the birds begin to sing,
but soon enough they leave,
taking their song with the warm breeze.
I wish for things to stay the same,
but I know everything is always evolving,
like the stars above.

????

Will the wind blow away your love?
Will you fall away from what you love the most?
Like the autumn leaves?
Will you say your gentle goodbyes?
Like flying geese?
Are you going to sugar coat all that you do?
Like a thin layer of snow?
When the ground freezes over,
will you bury your secrets far beneath the ice?
With each sunset will you come closer to leaving me behind?
The way the sun leaves the moon?

I Miss You

I miss you so, very much,
like the way the sun misses the moon.
I miss the way things were,
when you were here.

Like the way the land misses,
The warm, gentle blanket of summer-
in the dead of a long winter.

I miss the time I've lost with you,
Like the way the stars miss the moon,
On a peaceful new moon night.

I miss you so much.
The way I miss the winter,
on a hot summer evening.

Away

The sun takes away-
the moons sway,
In fear of what-
We'll say.
The wind speaks over-
us as if we were clovers,
that held no luck.

Section II

The sun, the moon, and the stars

Eerie Silence of Night

When the chaos of the day
gets washed away
and the serenity of night descends,
I begin to wonder, as the stars ascend.

Trying to put puzzle pieces together
that don't fit, stir my emotions like the weather.
The unknown bothers me.

I try to clear the hazy fog,
trying to find an answer in this misty sea.
I come to false conclusions,
trying to comfort my mind.

As all the words you've said, cruel and kind –
replay. Over and over and over again.
Until the sun rises,
Washing away the eerie silence of night.

The Things I Love

I love the beautiful stars,
that I cherish so much.

I love thunderstorms,
that I listen to so intently,
I love the peaceful sea,
that I enjoy so much.

I love the warm sun,
that I live happily under,
I love the gentle moon,
that I watch slowly change.

Daughter of the Moon

No matter the moon phase,
I know I'll feel it's gaze,
as I know the moon's energy,
is always with me.
It's gentle light a comfort,
one like no other.

A child of the night, I am.
Forever and always finding peace,
in the moons soft gaze, as I release-
all of the stress of today, bringing in-
a new perspective of tomorrow and today.

Keeping the ache that haunts my brain away,
I thank the moon's relaxing energy,
as I know no other comfort than the glow,
of the moon, that's light like snow.

Enchanted

Two complete opposites,
one as bright as the sun,
the other as peaceful as the moon.
Though they're almost never together,
when they meet, the sky becomes anomalous.

The moon, blocking the sun's blazing light,
To many, this eclipse is like a false night.
Serene, but ominous in many ways.
The sun doesn't mind the moon's shadow,
as it casts a spotlight on the moon.

Although their time together is short,
and their eclipse ends so soon,
They cherish their hours together.

The Moon's Love

My sun-
the only one,
I long for.
As the shore-
longs for the-
mysterious sea.
It's secrets a key-
to the space between-
Venus and stars.
Vast like a ravine,
where its secrets are ours.

The Sun's Love

My moon,
the only one,
I truly love.
The sea is soon-
to know the lone-
white singing doves,
Who hold the secrets of-
what is always above-
our heads in the space-
between the stars and Mars.
As we begin to freely race.

A Love They'll Never Have

The sun and the moon,
silently yearn for the other.
Yet, they only ever cross paths,
once in an enchanting eclipse.
They want a love they can never truly have.

Eclipse

Three years in between,
When a total eclipse can be seen.
The moon and sun meet,
Two halves made into a whole,
An eclipse is complete.

Cycle of Endings

With an ending,
A new beginning is revealed.
A constant cycle of rebirth,
an eclipse of emotions.

Always and Forever

I'll always be here for you,
sunrise to sunset,
new moon to full moon,
fall to spring,
summer to winter,
solar eclipse to lunar eclipse,

No matter what, I'll always be here.
Although, I may not show it often,
I love you the way-
I love the beautiful stars,
that I cherish so much.

Stars Above & Love

The stars above
know our love.
Written across the seas
like melodic keys.
Wind sweeps us away,
settling secrets with the day.
Whispers of the night
shine true
when the stars above-
see through,
knowing our love.

I'd Give you the Moon

If I could, I would give you the moon.
in hopes you wouldn't leave me *so* soon.
I would gift you what most chase,
and keep it forever in your grace.
When night falls, I'll gift you the stars,
and I'll call the night sky ours.

Soon enough, though, you'll push me away-
in the middle of rainy May.
And what more could I ever say?
This was bound to happen.

But I'll forever continue to sing;
If I could, I would give you the moon.
in hopes you wouldn't leave me *so* soon.

Enervated

Waiting for you,
Is like waiting for an eclipse.
With years of silence between us.
I try to grasp onto the light,
That shines above this sea.

But no matter how hard I try,
The total darkness of night,
Always brings memories back to me.

Every time I wait for you, I lie-
to myself, trying to replant the seeds-
of our relationship, but a relationship-
isn't a one way street,
and I don't need you to live,
so this is my bittersweet goodbye.

I refuse to water a plant that-
no longer wants to thrive.
I refuse to let the waters run high,
and overflow onto the shores,
leaving more of a mess for me to clean up.

I refuse to allow the sun to cover the moon.
As the peaceful night always ends too soon.

Watching the Sun Dance with the Moon

I watched the sun dance with the moon,
though everything stopped too soon,
The stars are not blind,
to what's on your mind,
as they always know,
our fates are set in the snow.
The sea will not just let you be,
as a shadow covers over its plea.

Ignorance Isn't Bliss

If only the stars could guide me,
far away from this terrible sea.
I'm sitting here, silently pleading,
all for you to notice what I've been saying.

I don't ask for the sun, the moon, and stars,
yet you act like it'll all be ours.
The rain hasn't yet washed away-
the feeling of despair from the day.

Yet you continue on as if nothings wrong.
I'm stuck in a pit of quicksand,
sinking lower and lower into the land,
wishing that it were the cold, icy snow.

Yet you act as if you're the one who knows.
Giving in to my fate, that'll turn to stone,
I silently wish the stars would guide me,
far away from this sea, so I can just be.

If I Wanted The Moon

If I had really wanted the moon,
would you still have left so soon?
You wanted the stars,
and I was willing to give you that *and* Mars.

If the sea wasn't so shallow,
would I still be a shadow
to you?
You, who's like the sun-
warm and welcoming but always on the run.

The Midnight Sky

Out of all of the stars in the sky,
You're the only one who caught my eye.
You shine brighter than the rest,
though, this feels like a cruel test,
I'll always find a way back to you,
and every word I speak is true,
I can always promise you that,
no matter where you're at,
I'll always find a way back to you.

And, out of all the stars in the sky,
You were the one to catch my eye.
You seemed to shine brighter than the rest,
and now I know it was a cruel test,
I have never felt so blue,
but what I felt was always true,
and no matter where you may be,
I'll always look for you, towards the sea.

Constellations?

The stars I notice first
will always have my heart.
Though, I take no part
in finding constellations.
I'll always look for the ones
I see first, on a new moon night,
when nothing but the stars' light
shines down onto the land.

Starry Eyed

Searching for something more,
The days pass me by,
like the wind on the shore.

I look to the stars for answers,
Hoping to see my future,
In their crystal like light.
As the darkness of night,
wraps around me like a blanket.
A constant reminder of reality.

I've let myself become starry eyed,
too engrossed in my dreams.
Always saying nothing is what it seems.
Always hoping for something unattainable.

I allow reality to set in, as I search-
for something new in the stars' light.
Now reaching for what's within reason,
instead of chasing after the next season.

A Sea of Mysteries

Wishes made on a shooting star,
Don't always come true.
Though, I am a dreamer,
Discourage finds its way to me.

Except, when I look up at the sea-
of stars, I am reminded of the unknown.
We don't know what lays upon the throne-
In the universe, up in the sea of stars.

What lays before us, is small compared-
To what we haven't yet found.

Stars

As peaceful as the gentle, quiet sea.
The stars are a guide to those who need it.
Their shimmering light shines down on the tree.
Their gentle light compared to the moonlit-
Sky is dull next to the glorious moon.
They light up the sky like a kid's night light.
Though, in the morning they leave far too soon,
They appear far too late into the night.
Lighting up the dull, gray, clear sky, they shine.
A confusing map engraved in the sky,
They never fail to tell me what is mine.
And, aloud, no one ever wonders why.
On depressing cloudy nights, I still look,
up at the sky as if it is a book.

The Gentle Stars

Stars, they shine the brightest-
when the moon is long gone.
The animals prefer the moon, though,
as it casts a gentle glow onto the land.
The stars, they aren't as grand-
as the beautiful moon, but that-
doesn't mean the stars aren't as beautiful.
When no clouds block the sky-
the sea reflects the stars-
barely noticeable to the blind eye.
Their light doesn't leave a brutal scar-
like the sun's so often does.

Losing Someone

Losing someone you love,
hollows out a part of you.
One day, you have them,
and the next,
you'll never see them again.
The realization stings,
worse than the sun's engulfing hug.
Worries begin to pile in your mind,
and only the moon will listen,
as you can only speak them aloud at night.
In the safety and comfort of the starlight.

Shooting Stars

As a child,
deep within my restless nights,
I'd sit by my window,
and hope for a shooting star.
The star that could grant any wish I had.
I would mistake a satellite
for a shooting star,
and wish for something small.
Something that has no value to me now.

As I've gotten older,
deep within my restless nights,
I go out onto my porch
and look up at the sky,
full of stars.
With no hopes of a shooting star,
The star I desperately wish
would come and grant me a wish.
I watch satellites move among the stars,
And although, I know better
I wish it were a shooting star,
that could grant one of my many wishes.

Wishes For the Future

I try to stay realistic,
but I wish upon the stars,
I am a mystic.

My wishes are dreams,
so close, yet so far.

I don't know the means-
of them all.

As my goals cannot fall,
like meteors,
that are mistaken for-
shooting stars,
that'll land on Mars.

Silly Wishes

Late into the night,
when things don't seem bright,
I wish upon a shooting star,
though, I am quite far-
from being a naïve child,
who believes in silly tales.
I allow myself to dream,
and let my hopes stream-
in, as I manifest my future.

Wish

When it's late at night,
and the stars shine bright,
I wish upon the light.
I wish for things I long for,
and things I have yet to yearn for.
The wind sings, cutting through the silence.
Giving the slumbering humans guidance.
In their dreams, they do not think it's the wind.
To them, it is something they haven't seen,
to them, it is something quite serene.
To me, it is a song of grace and sorrow,
similar to how the sea is far from shallow.
When I wish upon the gentle light,
I think of their hidden spite,
when I wish for things that don't feel right.

Longing

Once looked to the stars for answers,
Searching for a way out-
Now I'm filled with doubt.
Thought I knew my way,
But was left with dismay.

In the aftermath of it all,
I no longer wait for any call.
Ignoring the storms ahead,
I long for things that are now dead.

Meant to Be

Sometimes my thoughts are loud,
Almost like thunder.
Sometimes I wonder,
if the moon can hear them,
when it's late at night,
And the wind doesn't sing,
The sun cannot bring-
it's blazing, vivid light,
To cover the moon's gentle night.
The stars can agree,
they know what's meant to be.
Is it truly meant to be, if we can't see?
Or so the sun says.

Turning Nothing Into Something

The sun makes a fool out of the moon.
All of its jokes were said with malicious intent.
The sea watches this happen, it knows it's wrong,
but does the fun have to stop so soon?
The stars fade into a beautiful nothing,
as the sunlight rises,
and turns nothing into something.

Nonsense?

If the stars could guide me
away from this sea,
I would follow them gratefully.
I would use the sky as a map.
Not worrying if it's a trap,

The stars are my guide, after all.
And they will not fall
like the autumn leaves.
Instead, they are strong like trees.
And I say this with ease.

The stars rest in the sky
where clouds fly high.
They look down at me
as they stare at the sea.
They look on the rest of the land,
but they don't understand–
Why I am stranded in this sea of sand.

And again I think to myself,
"If the stars could guide me
away from this sea,
I would follow them gratefully.
I would use the sky as a map.
Not worrying if it's a trap."

Day Falls to Night

When day falls to night,
forget the pain of the sun.
Remember the vibrant light,
that you didn't need to run from.
Remember the warmth,
will always keep you close,
as the star that leads you north,
will take you to the coast,
where the sky meets the sea.

Yule

On this day,
the sun's rays
set earlier
as darkness
engulfs the land.
The stars' light
glimmers off the
wintery sand.
This year, the New Moon
is on its way
and only two days away,
from the return of the sun.

Section III

Time

Fate

Many say fate is set in stone,
like hieroglyphs hung up on walls.
That tells stories to all.

Some say fate is crystal clear,
That it's something not to fear.
Some say fate is merciful,
that it'll create something beautiful.

Fate, though, is simply fate.
Something that cannot be defined,
Something that cannot be underlined,
or tamed, like the way the weather-
listens to no one, as if its a feather,
that falls through the air with grace.

The Small Things

I try to notice things others wouldn't,
but sometimes it's as hard as finding a certain star
in the night sky full of millions that reflect like a
mirror.

Although, for all the small things I take note of,
I appreciate them with all of my heart.
Even if it's just saying 'I love you' at random,
I enjoy these small moments humans have,
ones we never seem to cherish, as life seems long,
but in reality it's short, as time waits for no one.

It seems as if we take these moments of love
for granted because we believe we always have
more time,
and for all the small things I notice,
they'll fill my life with more warmth than it may
appear.

A Little Less Wiser

I'm getting older,
and a little less wiser.
Each day ticks by,
and I don't cherish every moment.

My favorite season's chilly sigh-
is cast upon my cheeks as I look up-
at the cloudy sky, that warns us of a storm.

My thoughts are a storm that's brewing.
The more time I waste standing here,
not truly living every second, worrying-
over small things that'll be inconvenient soon,
the less time I have with those who I love dearly,
like the moon.

Inevitable Change

The moon is forever changing,
Never staying the exact same-
for more than a day.

As if it changes its mind everyday.
I am like the moon.
Though, my phases last months.
I've come to realize that I'm more like the seasons,
I change little by little, never drastically without
reason.

I don't think I'm the same star I was yesterday,
I've lost the spot in the sky I once took up.
Now you can only remember where the star-
May have been, unless a photo turns up.

It's kind of funny, how slowly I change,
But how quickly it feels months later,
When noticing I'll never be the same,
As I was eight months ago.
And now I've began to realize,
In the next two months I'll change.

I will never be the same as I am today,
and that's okay.

Memories Veiled in Ivory

Letting something else fill the void,
With silence as loud as winter.
The words stuck in my mind like a splinter.
I'll keep my memory attached Polaroids,
Refusing to let go just yet.

Time will go on, though, and the sun will set,
And eventually I'll forget,
As even the seasons let go,
Allowing the leaves to fall,
With time bringing in the snow.

I'll try to remember it all,
Treasuring each memory,
As if it's veiled in ivory.

What Once Was

Looking up at the stars,
I think of what would've been ours.
I like to think fate isn't set in stone,
but late at night, when I'm alone,
I reminisce on what once was.
Though, there'll never be a because,
I'll imagine what could've been.
I'll recall those days when-
the sun shone a little brighter,
and the clouds were a little bit lighter.
The days when the waters weren't as high,
and the limit was always the sky.

A Release of Time

In the quiet moments of my past,
I think of what will last.
The future is a known mystery,
one I wish I knew like history.

What scares me isn't the setting sun,
it's the way that time runs.
Dancing around me like the seasons,
It changes its reasons,
prolonging a dreadful winter,
Or a humid summer,
we're stuck with, like a splinter.

Time does as it pleases,
keeping its grip on us; with no sign of release.

Promises of Time

Time is a fickle thing,
never in one spot twice.
Always on the run,
playing a wicked game,
with the mortals it torments.
It whispers sweet riddles,
melodies as soothing as a fiddle.

It makes promises worth more than gold,
but you'll quickly find they just turn to mold.
Time isn't a sinister being,
though, it doesn't care, either.

The setting sun is a natural clock,
the sand falling down the hourglass,
ticking away the years Time has given you.

Time isn't something to dance with for-
once you take its hand, it'll whisk you away.
Spinning you around and around until you're gray.

Waiting For Time

A strange thing, time is.
as long as the wind sings,
it'll quicken, shortening the song.
When the wind silences, it'll slow-
and the silence is stretched out far too long-
but Time doesn't mind, as it dances,
to its own uneven rhythm.

Dancing with anything and everything-
Time chooses the tempo, as it ticks by.
In the winter, you can hear it sigh-
as it tangles itself up with the trees,
the elaborate dance showing no sign of stopping.
In the summer, you can hear it fly,
as it dances with the bright, warm sun.
Its speed is not far from a run.

In the fall, you can hear it lie-
as it quickly sweeps up the autumn leaves,
with little to no care in the world.
In the spring, you can hear it cry,
as the rain ignores the Time's pace,
pelting the land to its own rhythm.

Time is a strange thing,
as it waits for no one and nothing,
though, everything waits for it.

A Cursed Truth

The saying 'you don't know what you have until it's gone,'
is a truth that feels like a weighted curse, one you'll never be rid of.
Seasons change quicker than we realize, as winter holds fall close,
and spring practically dances with summer as light is "saved."

Day chases the night, as night chases the day, stuck in an infinite loop.
Most mortal's don't notice, or perhaps they just don't care,
as time dances around the universe, letting us go while holding us close,
we focus on little things that won't matter in a week, in a month.

We know there's few absolutes in life, the most intimidating one,
is something many fear, causing us to be blind to the present.
Though, death still looms above us, and whisks those we love away.
it's not until then, that we notice what we have, or rather, what we had.

Once death rips something away from us, we'll never get it back,
and that's when we realize what we lack.
We don't truly acknowledge what we have until it's gone,
always believing we will have more time, more memories,
but we know the truth, time cannot be prolonged or borrowed.

Unwise

The sun will rise,
no matter how unwise-
I may be, wishing for it-
to be still for one moment.

What's The Point?

I've watched the seasons change,
one day it's beautifully cold winter,
and the next it's a humid summer.
I've watched everyone around me change.
As they become the person they are now.
And there's no going back in time.
I think of the forever changing moon.
As my new normal leaves all too soon.
One day, it's a lovely autumn day,
and the next the rain washes it away,
as spring begins her reign on the land.
The next day brings summer and her sand.
I long for the past, and the unimaginable future,
But what's the point?
Summer only comes once a year,
and only once a year does Fall celebrate.
Winter only reigns once every year.
And Spring only paints the land once.
What's the point of wishing for the future?
When I can enjoy the swift breeze of fall,
as she begins to settle in, and summer leaves.
As distant Winter begins to weave,
a new story for the land, and its people.
As Spring begins to plan her next painting.
I've watched the seasons change,
and I claim to enjoy them all,
as everything is forever changing like the moon.

The Stories in Lines

In each person, there's a story,
one you may or may not know,
but in every person,
there are hints of their long story,
such as in their beauty.
Around their mouth,
some may have lines,
showing the smiles they have given
and the laughs they have had.
Some may have lines
at the corner of their eyes,
showing their years of laughter,
showing their moments of joy.
Some may have creases in their brow,
showing their times of surprise
or their times of confusion.
There are many great stories,
even in very simple lines.

Unimaginative

For every word I can't say,
I try to write it down,
but at the end of the day,
I know I'll never find the words.
They jumble together,
like the sunset's melting colors.
For every excuse I make,
I know what it'll take.
Time.

However, I'm impatient.
I wish the words would flow,
like a stream going into a river.
And for every thing I wish for,
I know I'll be tired always,
hoping for better words than before.

Time

Time is something we all want more of,
something we can never get our hands on.
Time is something I want more of.
Something I cannot grasp.
Lately time has passed by quicker,
a minute is a second,
an hour is a minute,
and a day feels more like a few hours.

When I think back to what I did last month,
almost everything I did feels like yesterday.
When I recall memories from my childhood,
the years that have passed since then,
hit me like a punch to the gut.
It feels like only yesterday I was in 5th grade,
with little to no cares in the world.

Now I am older,
with responsibilities and expectations to meet.
I wish I could slow down time,
so I can enjoy every moment more.
Time may be something I will never get enough of,
but I will always hope and wish for more.

Like Snow

Wishing for the past,
Knowing the present won't last.
It'll disappear like the snow.
One moment it's all you know,
The next it's gone as if it never was.

Past, Present, and Future

Past; The Fool
A new journey awaits me,
drawing me to the unknown,
like a magnet to the sea.
Whatever is thrown-
my way, I'll accept with joy.

Present; The World (reversed)
Destroyed, time moves on.
The past is set in stone,
like glass that reflects dawn.
I yearn for the outgrown-
past, that I love so dear.
I wish I could go back to that year.
Time moves so fast, I feel-
As if it's slipping through-
my fingers like sand.

Future; The Sun
Although, time skips past me,
There is no guarantee that-
I won't find something better at sea.
Life is an hourglass,
The sand slipping through our fingers.
One day, though, a memory will surpass-
My treasured past.

Section IV

A variety

The Little Things I Favor

I love the feeling of a rainy day,
when the air is frigid,
and everything feels gloomy.
I love sitting next to the bay,
listening to the waves crash against the shore,
as I read in the cool shade, on the sand.
I love taking photos.
I find beauty in everything,
especially nature and the sky.
I love listening to music,
anywhere from loud, heavy metal
to soft, upbeat pop music.
I love giving others tarot readings,
the way I can read a handful of cards with ease,
the art on each card capturing my eye.
I love how poetry can be heart-wrenching,
with deep, heartfelt meanings,
but it can be happy and joyful, too.
I love writing,
and how freeing it is;
There is no limit to my imagination.

An Answer of Why

"Why do the small things matter to you?"
I've never been asked this question,
but I've thought about it numerous times.
Why do they?
Well, because I love the way the moon-
Gives the stars their own time to shine,
on a new moon night when there's no light.
It's something small that occurs every month.
Yet, it matters to me all the same like the way-
Listening to music with my family matters.
In the car, connected through a song
Though, it's only a few minutes long,
unlike winter, which I love so dearly.
Its icy hugs engulf me as the snow falls,
Painting a picture I hold dear to me.
Though it's not the only one,
I hold pictures of the places I'd like to go dear to me-
The way I hold my love for dogs.
If I could, I'd take in every stray,
Casting their pain away.
But why?
Why do these 'small' things matter to me?
Well, because they just do.

Home

For the longest time,
I thought home was a place.
I thought it was a house,
in the small state I live in.
I assumed it had to be a place,
one I was bound to by invisible forces.
I assumed I was only homesick
when I was far from that place.
Except, to me, home isn't a place.
It's a small group of people: my family.
I know now I can move anywhere in the world,
and never feel 'at home' unless I'm with my family.

Unspoken Words

There's things we've left unspoken,
though, there isn't a doubt in my mind,
we say everything and nothing at all-
in the small gestures we make.

I Love You

What more do I have to say?
I may not speak it aloud,
but I do love you,
and no rain could wash away-
the love I have come to know for you.

I'll Cherish Your Love

I'll cherish your love,
as nothing lasts forever.
Gone in the wind with the dove-
our love will fade to nothing,
like the sunsets I cherish so dearly.
At night, I see much more clearly.
With the stars as my guide,
they lead me away from the tide,
and deeper into the sea.

To Be Loved

To be loved means to be engulfed-
in a warm blanket, even when the cold-
tries to seep into your bones.
To be loved means to be seen,
as a person who makes mistakes,
as someone who is perfectly human.

A Love That'll Last

I want a love that'll last,
one where we're as old as the sun,
and neither of us will have to run,
as we dance around our fears.

I want a love, who'll travel the world with me.
Where we will happily spend years-
together, walking on a beach next to a new sea.

I want a love, who'll write me small poems-
the way I would for them.
I want a love, who'll listen to music with me.
So we can sing along, with no care in the world.

I want a love, who'll find the beauty in everything.
From the sunsets, to a small buzzing bee.
From the way someone smiles or the way the leaves
curl.

I want a love that'll truly last.

Those I Love

I've come to realize,
I am not solely myself.
I am pieces of those I love,
Pieces of those I've loved, too.
They make me who I am,
who I strive to become.

Deep in my heart,
I know there's not a single part-
of me that hasn't been seen,
by someone I've loved, and like a dream,
my memories become hazier over time.

There's still those silly things I say,
That reminds me of that old friend of mine.
The one I no longer talk to.
There's still those songs I listen to,
only because my family liked them.

Every now and then, they remind me of my home.
There's still those places I reminisce about,
places filled with memories I long for.

Photography

Photos; they capture memories,
moments, too, that you cherish,
keeping them preserved forever.
A fond moment stuck in time?
Now stuck in colorful ink on paper.
A memory you'll soon forget?
Months, years, decades later,
It's still there, reminding you of—
a fond memory that's one of many—
that you've slowly forgotten.
A sunset so beautiful, that's unlike any other?
In a photo, its beauty is preserved,
in a portrait, painted by the light.
Photos; they remind you of the good,
and sometimes, the forgotten.

Ominous

Folk story,
Moon of doom,
Soon bonds bloom,
Color of glory,
Storms roll on,
Sword of story.
Flood on down,
Toll of frowns.
Fond of wrong,
Whorl so long,
Roof of horror,
Fog swoops on,
Growls of doom.
Fools go on,
Ghosts of frost,
Howls of moss.

A Star's Disappearance

If a star disappears,
Would anyone notice?
One less light in the sky,
one less star out of trillions.
If a star loses its spark,
Would you even bat an eye?
One star, dimmer than the rest.
One dim star, out of trillions.
If there were only a handful of-
stars would you care more?

The Veil Between

It's easy to ignore what lays beyond,
in the veil between the light and the dark.
I am not afraid of what may lurk.
I am afraid of what will be left,
as nothing is as simple as being erased.
There'll be pieces left to be put together.
A puzzle forever unfinished, never meant-
to be finished, forever a mystery to resent.
Answers will come, but nothing will stay-
in place as the years pass. Like a bay,
what lays beyond will engulf the puzzle,
and all you're left with is a mystery to nuzzle.

You're Not The Sun

Must the wind sing-
for you to listen?
Must the water glisten-
for it to catch your eye?
If I am the night,
you aren't the light.
You don't outshine;
those who don't whine.
You are not the sun,
to those who run-
longer marathons than you.

An Ocean of Emotion

We feel in such a deep way,
flooding our veins throughout the day.
Some let themselves feel,
then move on, as if it wasn't a big deal.
Some cling onto their emotions,
causing commotions.
Some push it away,
avoiding what they can't say.
Our feelings are a vast sea,
one that some try to flee-
from, one that some sink in.
One that some welcome in.

Failing To See

Wishing is a silly thing to do,
and yet, I continue to do so.
I wish for impossible things,
but, to me, they seem so close.
My rose colored sunglasses are on,
though, unrequited love isn't-
what I'm failing to see.
I wish, and wish, and wish, and wish,
and all for the same, foolish things.
The stars sparkle above, but never show-
me my fate; my set in stone future.
Though, they give nothing away,
I'll continue to wish, and seek them-
for guidance; forever wishing for something more.

Too Different

We're too different,
bound to never work.
You are the sun,
and I am the moon.
We will only create an eclipse.
Casting nocturnal light everywhere.

What More?

Winter turns to spring,
and night turns to day.
What more do I have to say?
To try to change your mind?
I know my words aren't as tasteful as sweet wine,
but do take my words into consideration.

What You Couldn't Say

Your words were like a false sea,
only meant to convince me.
And when I asked what it'd be,
you still decided to go with the wind,
Foolishly I still waited, until eventually,
I grew tired of waiting for you,
and with each passing day,
I knew what you couldn't say.

Eyes

You don't need to speak the words aloud,
for your eyes already tell me the story.
And, for all of its glory,
I'd rather be stuck in a large crowd,
then be blinded by your imaginary clouds.

A Hazy Heart

Sand falls apart-
quicker than my heart.
Not even the suns-
Burning gaze-
Lifts the haze-
that surrounds my eyes.
It hides what lies-
Beyond the mossy stone
walls of this broken land.

Why?

All I ever ask is 'why?'
Why don't you try?
Why am I the only one,
on this two way street?
Why must you ignore me?
Why can't two sides meet?
Why do I bother even asking at all?
And even after everything,
All I ever ask is 'why?'

You

This game has gone on for too long,
I'm tired of being the one to run,
after someone who thinks they do no wrong.
You think you shine as bright as the sun,
but I think your words burn more.
You aren't gentle like the sea,
as you like to claim, to lure-
me back into your cold embrace.
I'm tired of running this race,
where I know I'll never win.
You gave me hope when I needed it the most,
and then ripped it away when I began-
to trust you with all of my wretched heart.

A Final Goodbye

Leave me like the setting sun,
your love's shown in the sky,
our final goodbye.
Whispers of your name-
follow me around like a game.
Reminders of you are everywhere.
I know one day they'll go away,
But how long until I get there?
I once enjoyed the warmth of the day,
I no longer do, though.
It reminds me of the words you'd sow-
together; carefully crafted just for me.
Memories of you flood my mind like the sea.
But there's nowhere for me to run.

Once Had

Missing a version of you,
One I thought I once knew.
I fell in love, and didn't think twice.
You were the moon to me,
Pulling me in like the sea.
It feels like a twist of fate,
Like the universe rolled a pair of dice.
Your words weren't full of hate,
Yet they hurt as if they were.
My vision begins to blur,
As I think of memories with you.
Though, I wouldn't change a thing,
And even though remembering stings,
I'm reminded of the love I once had.

Too Much

Sometimes I wonder,
If I love *too* much.
If being loved by me,
Feels more like drowning in a sea.
Rather than basking in the sun's warmth.

Never A Mistake

I've been told that loving someone is never a mistake,
That loving someone who couldn't wasn't a waste,
That it shows how emotionally mature I am.
But it feels like my heart has stopped beating,
As if it's been ripped out of my chest,
And replaced with an empty void.
One that's slowly made me a little paranoid.

I've thought over every touch, every shared look.
Wondering where it all went wrong.
Wondering when things had changed,
Wondering how I could've prevented this pain.

Words replaying in my mind,
Over and over and over and over again.
I loved, with all of my heart,
I thought I knew my feelings were shared.
In the end, though, I loved someone who couldn't love me.
It felt like a *mistake*.
It felt like a *waste*.
Now, though, I'm glad I loved,
As, for me, loving someone is never a waste,
Because it shows how much *I* cared.

Forgiveness

Sometimes, it's easier to forgive,
than to hold a long lasting grudge.
It makes it easier to live,
without a burden to judge.
It's not easy to always let it go,
but to keep my peace,
I won't forgive just for show.

Haunted

We all have a shadow
that follows us around,
never leaving our sides.
It's like a lost puppy,
one that trails behind us.
Except, we forget it's there,
so it's more like the slight chill
in the air on cool autumn days.
We get so used to our shadow,
that we forget it's even there.

Expectations aren't our shadows:
we don't always forget about them.
They follow us everywhere,
always in our line of sight,
constantly making themselves known.
Expectations are more like winter.
They freeze over our paths,
making us slip on the icy path of life.
They make us forget how warm we are,
covering us in a blanket of bitter air.

If Only You'd Listen

If only you would truly listen,
If only you'd see the water glisten,
If only you'd see the beauty of the moon,
If only you'd stop leaving me so soon.

Depths of Your Mind

It never truly goes away,
it'll still whisper in the wind,
in the depths of your mind.
Like waves that quiet the bay.
It'll make a home in your mind.

Death

I hope death feels like the moon;
a gentle reminder I am not infinite.
A reminder that my years are limited,
and I may leave far too soon.

The Silence of Death

Deep into a bloody war,
when time begins to slow,
you can hear the Valkyrie's loud roar.
The sound so beautifully terrifying, you know-
they've come to collect many souls.
The outcome of this war is in their hands.
They whisk away the spirits of those who are no longer.
As they soar through the night, far above the land.
As they begin to leave, they leave a trail-
of colored light a major detail,
you cannot ignore, as their battle cries,
begin to turn to sighs.
The silence of death becomes loud,
as the chilly night air warns-
Valkyrie's cries are not weightless like a cloud.
They'll be back, as war is an uncontrollable storm.

A Midnight Stroll

Deep into the forest,
when wolves howl at the moon-
you'll be wanting to leave soon.
Midnight is on your doorstep,
as you take your time, strolling-
through the hours of night,
as if the moon's sinister light-
will protect you from blood thirsty-
monsters that roam the land.
As the stars come out, sparkling like sand,
the trees shift into dark shadows,
reaching for a soul to prey on.
The sun's warmth is long gone,
yet this midnight stroll has not come to an end.

A Kingdom of Darkness

As a storm rolls in,
Something sinister begins-
to stir as the land cools,
preparing for the ruthless winter.
Beings of the unknown come out to play,
as the wind pushes the leaves away.
 Night dawns upon the land quicker,
as bats roam the dark, moonless sky.
A kingdom of darkness, it is.
With a Queen and King of pale moonlight-
To guide the creatures of the night,
vampires roam the land when the sun slumbers.
Their Kingdom of Darkness will forever live on-
until the Sun and Moon make amends,
stopping their foolish eons long fight.

Castle of Midnight

When night descends onto the land,
monsters terrorize the once peaceful minds-
of the souls who inhabit the Earth.
The wind screeches as it dances through-
a vacant castle, once full of happy warmth,
now cold and unforgiving, as its haunted halls-
are decorated, dreary portraits that are full of dust,
hang on the walls.

Spirits roam the castle, forever searching for their loves,
who are forever lost to the wind, never to be found again.
Their loves they'll never know again until the sun truly meets the moon.
Gorgons protect the castle, keeping it safe from prying eyes.
Though, that's not their only job. They keep the spirits locked away,
forever hiding them in the castle that sits atop a lone mountain.

The Castle of Midnight hides secrets of the innocent,
of the guilty, of the poor, and of the wealthy.
Once a soul enters the cursed castle,
they shall never walk out with all of their soul.

A price is paid to step foot into the Castle of Midnight.
Some whisper it's a game, one so cursed your soul is the price,
some whisper it's all a hoax, a figment of your imagination.

Though, you'll never truly know, until you step foot into the castle,
ready to dance away eternity with the longing spirits of old.

The Sea, The Monster & The Night

The sea, black as night.
Quiet waves gently hit the shore, making music like
an instrument.
The stars are a night light, dimly lighting
everything.

Creatures lurk beneath.
The water holds secrets, only the stars can keep.
The moon watches carefully.
Owls cry out a warning.

The monster that lurks beneath knows when they'll
come storming.
It *watches*.
And, waits for an unexpecting victim.

The moon, the stars, and the animals all watch.
When nothing approaches,
the water still holds its secrets,
the stars, the animals, and the moon keep quiet,
waiting.

The Valkyrie's Armor of Light

Into the heart of war,
Valkyries ride, as they soar-
above the land of mass bloodshed.
Whisking away the souls of the dead,
bringing them to the magnificent Valhalla.
As they ride in glory, the reflection of light-
bounces off of their armor in the night.
To the mortals who look up at the sky,
they realize it is no longer pitch black,
as lights of blue, green, and purple paint-
the sky above into something far from faint.
The warriors ride on, casting the sky aglow,
as a war rages on feet below.

What's Above

I could've gave you the sun,
so you'd never have to worry
I would've given you the stars.
And I'd call everything ours,
Whatever you wanted, Love.
But, what is above,
Is not ours to take.
And all for your sake,
I couldn't take the lovely moon.
You would've left me far too soon.

This Sea of Voices

"You have a voice, use it," they say.
So I do, but my words get lost in
the sea of voices that surround me.
I repeat myself, louder this time,
trying to swim to the surface
of this sea of voices.
No one hears a single word.
So I swim closer to the surface
of this noisy, murky sea.
I repeat myself once again,
my fingers almost touching
the chilly air above the sea.
No one hears me.
So I give up, and let myself sink
back into this neglectful, noisy sea.
When the moon finally notices
the creatures that lurk in this murky sea,
it says, "I'm sorry, I didn't hear you."
I can feel their words burn through
the cold freezing waters of the sea I swim in.
The moon would've heard the creatures if it had
listened.
They would've heard me if they had listened to me.

www.ingramcontent.com/pod-product-compliance
Lightning Source LLC
LaVergne TN
LVHW092047060526
838201LV00047B/1279